Zoo Math

Zoo Patterns

Patricia Whitehouse

Heinemann Library
Chicago, Illinois

Customer Service 888-454-2279
Visit our website at www.heinemannlibrary.com

Designed by Sue Emerson/Heinemann Library and Ginkgo Creative, Inc.
Printed and bound in the U.S.A. by Lake Book

06 05 04
10 9 8 7 6 5 4 3 2

Library of Congress Cataloging-in-Publication Data
Whitehouse, Patricia, 1958-
   Zoo patterns / Patricia Whitehouse.
      p. cm. — (Zoo math)
Includes index.
Summary: An introduction to the concept of patterns, using examples from the coats and feathers of zoo animals.
   ISBN: 1-58810-550-4 (HC), 1-58810-758-2 (Pbk.)
    1. Pattern perception—Juvenile literature. 2. Zoo animals—Juvenile literature. [1. Pattern perception.
   2. Zoo animals.] I. Title.
   BF294 .W45 2002
   152.14'23—dc21
   153.7'52—dc21
               2001004901

Acknowledgments
The author and publishers are grateful to the following for permission to reproduce copyright material:
p. 4 Alan Paterson; p. 5 Frank Lane Picture Agency/Corbis; pp. 6, 8, 10, 12 PhotoDisc; p. 7 Mark Allen Stack/Tom Stack & Associates; p. 9 Eda Rogers; p. 11 W. Wayne Lockwood, M.D./Corbis; p. 13 Ron Austing/Cincinnati Zoo; pp. 14, 15 Jim Gray/Stock Photography; pp. 16, 17 Paul Souders; p. 18 Kennan Ward/Corbis; p. 19 Papilio/Corbis; pp. 20, 21 Anthony Mercieca/Photophile/Stock Photography; pp. 22, 24 Cathy and Gordon ILLG.

Cover photograph by PhotoDisc

Every effort has been made to contact copyright holders of any material reproduced in this book. Any omissions will be rectified in subsequent printings if notice is given to the publisher.

Special thanks to our advisory panel for their help in the preparation of this book:

Eileen Day, Preschool Teacher
Chicago, IL

Paula Fischer, K–1 Teacher
Indianapolis, IN

Sandra Gilbert,
Library Media Specialist
Houston, TX

Angela Leeper,
Educational Consultant
North Carolina Department
of Public Instruction
Raleigh, NC

Pam McDonald,
Reading Teacher
Winter Springs, FL

Melinda Murphy,
Library Media Specialist
Houston, TX

Helen Rosenberg, MLS
Chicago, IL

Anna Marie Varakin,
Reading Instructor
Western Maryland College

We would like to thank the Brookfield Zoo in Brookfield, Illinois, for reviewing this book for accuracy.

Some words are shown in bold, **like this.**
You can find them in the picture glossary on page 23.

Contents

What Makes a Pattern?

Patterns are shapes and colors that repeat.

There are patterns on things, like this crosswalk.

There are patterns on animals, too.

This **toucan** has stripes on its **beak**.

What Animal Has Black and White Stripes?

Here is its hair.

The black and white stripes make a pattern.

This animal runs fast.

It is a **zebra.**

What Animal Is Gold with Black Stripes?

Here is its hair.

The gold hair and black stripes make a pattern.

Look at the long, striped tail.

It is a tiger.

What Animal Is Tan with Brown Spots?

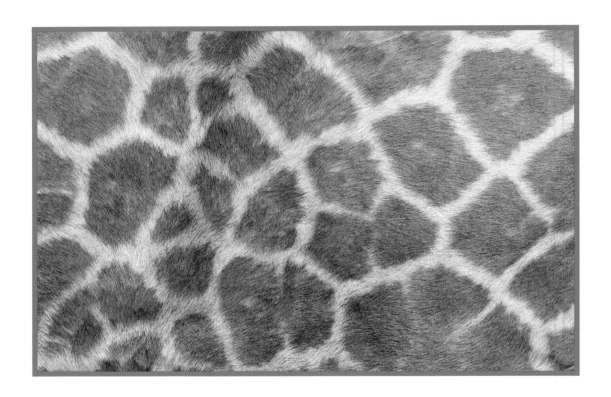

Here is its hair.

The brown spots on the tan fur make a pattern.

The spots go up its long neck.

It is a giraffe.

What Animal Is Yellow with Black Spots?

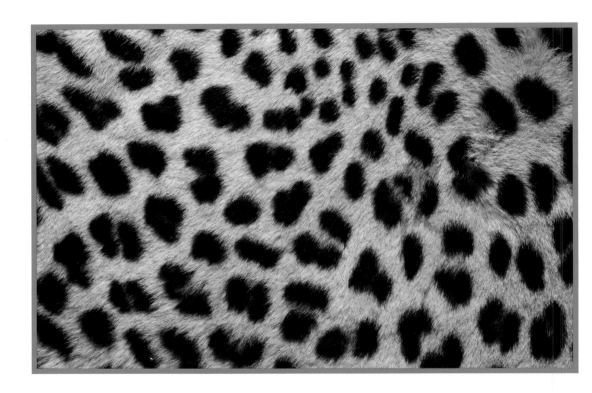

Here is its hair.

The black spots make a pattern on the yellow fur.

There are a few spots on its head.

It is a **cheetah**.

What Animal Is Tan with Black Circles?

Here is its hair.

The black circles on the tan fur make a pattern.

There are black circles on its tail, too.

It is a **jaguar**.

What Animal Is Brown with Brown Spots?

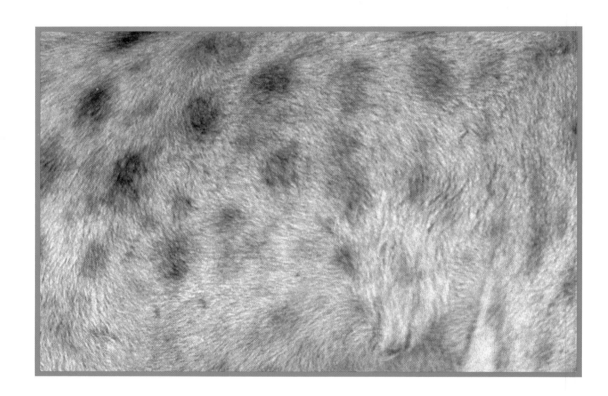

Here is its hair.

The brown spots on the brown fur make a pattern.

This animal's name comes from the sound it makes.

It is a **laughing hyena.**

What Animal Has Spots and Stripes?

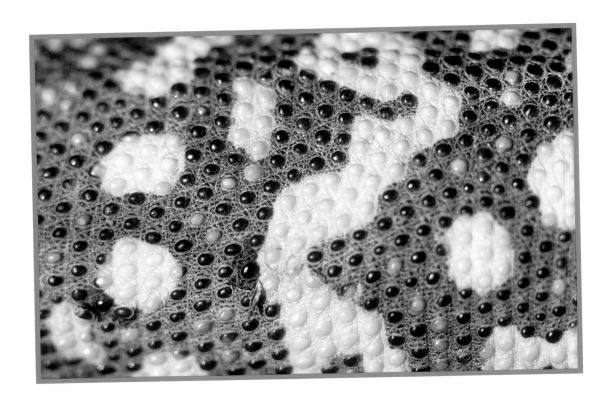

Here is its skin.

The spots and stripes make a pattern.

It has stripes on its tail and spots on its back.

It is a **Gila monster.**

What Animal Has Diamonds?

Here is its skin.

The **diamond** shapes make a pattern.

This animal's tail can make noise.

It is a **rattlesnake.**

What Animal Am I?

I am a bird.

The pattern on my tail looks like eyes.

Look for the answer on page 24.

Picture Glossary

beak
page 5

jaguar
(JAG-war)
page 15

rattlesnake
page 21

cheetah
page 13

laughing hyena
(LAFF-ing hi-EE-na)
page 17

toucan
(TOO-kan)
page 5

diamond
page 20

peacock
page 24

zebra
page 7

Gila monster
(HE-la mon-stur)
page 19

Note to Parents and Teachers

Recognizing patterns is a key math skill. *Zoo Pairs* introduces children to the concept using the patterns found on the hair, skin, or feathers of zoo animals. As you read the book together, cover the photo on each right-hand page with a piece of paper. Show children the pattern on the left-hand page and ask them to predict the animal that has this type of pattern. Keep the picture on the right-hand side covered as you read the third sentence. Then uncover the picture to reveal the animal. Were the children's predictions correct? Younger children can practice making patterns. Go back to the striped crosswalk on page 4, then set out a simple pattern of plastic blocks in two different colors. After you've established the pattern, ask children to tell you which color should come next. Later, children can practice making patterns and asking you to tell them which color should come next.

Index

Answer to quiz on page 22

I am a **peacock**.